OCT 01

Fields in Sa Pa, In The Highest Mountains Of Vietnam

FACES
AND
PLACES

VIETNAM

BY PATRICK MERRICK

THE CHILD'S WORLD®, INC.

GRAPHIC DESIGN AND PRODUCTION
Robert E. Bonaker / Graphic Design & Consulting Co.

PHOTO RESEARCH
James R. Rothaus / James R. Rothaus & Associates

PHOTOGRAPHY
Cover photo: Portrait of a young Vietnamese girl
by ©Catherine Karrow/CORBIS

Library of Congress Cataloging-in-Publication Data
Merrick, Patrick.
Vietnam / by Patrick Merrick.
p. cm.
Includes index.
Summary: Introduces the history, geography, people, and
customs of the Southeast Asian country of Vietnam.
ISBN 1-56766-740-6 (lib. reinforced : alk. paper)

1. Vietnam — Juvenile literature.
[1. Vietnam] I. Title.

DS556.3 .M47 2000
915.97 — dc21   99-054116

Table of Contents

Where Is Vietnam?

When you look outside, you might see many different things. You could be looking at forests, deserts, mountains, or lakes. From close-up, everywhere seems like such a wonderful and different place to live. However, if you took a flight in an airplane, the farther up you went, you would find that the differences are not so great, and that we all live on the same planet— Earth. Finally, from the

Western Hemisphere

Eastern Hemisphere

Space Shuttle, Earth looks like a beautiful green and blue place to live. The first thing that you might notice from space is that Earth is mostly covered with water.

Vietnam (white) Is In The East And U.S.A. (green) Is In The West

In this water, you would see large areas of land called **continents**. The largest of these continents is Asia. There are many fascinating countries in Asia. One of these countries is called Vietnam.

Arctic Ocean

NORTH AMERICA

United States of America

EUROPE

ASIA

Atlantic Ocean

Pacific Ocean

Pacific Ocean

AFRICA

Vietnam

SOUTH AMERICA

Indian Ocean

AUSTRALIA

The World Shown Flat

ANTARCTICA

CHINA

MYANMAR

LAOS

Gulf of Tonkin

THAILAND

SOUTH CHINA SEA

VIETNAM

Adaman Sea

CAMBODIA

Gulf of Thailand

INDIAN OCEAN

Close-Up of Vietnam

An Oyster Fishing Village In Thua Thein Province

• Sa Pa
• Moc Chau

THUA THEIN PROVINCE

MEKONG DELTA

The
Land

A Muong Village In Moc Chau

Vietnam is a long, skinny country with much of it's land touching the South China Sea. If you use your imagination, Vietnam looks like the letter *S*. Most of Vietnam is filled with beautiful mountains or hills. In fact, the mountains in Vietnam run through the country and into the sea! In the sea, the mountains form hundreds of tiny islands.

Besides the mountains, Vietnam is covered with thick jungles and forests. Within these jungles, thousands of rivers and streams flow to the sea.

In the north and south of the country are large **deltas**, or flat areas of land. These deltas were created by huge rivers that emptied into the sea. Because of their rich, flat land and all the water, the delta areas are used for farming.

Finally, if you like water and beaches, Vietnam has many beautiful areas of white sand and warm winds. Within Vietnam's borders, people live in many types of places.

Rice Fields On The Mekong Delta

Plants & Animals

Because there are so many different types of land, there are many different types of plants and animals. Thanks to Vietnam's warm, moist weather, you can find all kinds of plants. There are tropical forests, swamp forests, coconut palms, exotic fruit trees, and large areas of tall, sharp grasses. However, most of the forests are quickly disappearing because of **deforestation** and poor farming techniques.

Vietnam's remaining forests, however, are alive with interesting animals. You can find elephants, snakes, tigers, leopards, bears, and monkeys. In the water, crocodiles, turtles, seals, and dolphins swim with brightly colored fish. Vietnam is now trying to save these animals' homes so these fascinating creatures do not die out.

CORBIS/Steve Raymer

A Muong Man Riding An Elephant In Ban Don

Water Buffalo Along A River On The Red Delta

RED
DELTA

• Ban Don

MEKONG
DELTA

CORBIS/Owen Franken

Palm
Trees Along
A River On The
Mekong
Delta

The Cham
Towers At
Quy Nhon
Were Used
For Worship

Quy Nhon

Long Ago

There have been people living in Vietnam for thousands of years. Because of its position, many countries have tried to take over Vietnam. A long time ago, China conquered the Vietnamese people and controlled the country for 1,000 years. The Vietnamese finally took back their country from China. Eventually, France conquered the country and ruled it until 1954.

Again the Vietnamese regained their independence through fighting. However, this time the country was split into two parts, North Vietnam and South Vietnam. Soon the two sides started fighting each other, and a terrible war began. The war lasted a long time. Many countries, including the United States, fought in the war between 1954 and 1975.

Eventually, North Vietnam won the war. During the fighting, more than 3 million people died, and many parts of the country were destroyed. In the end, Vietnam was finally one independent country again, but at a terrible cost.

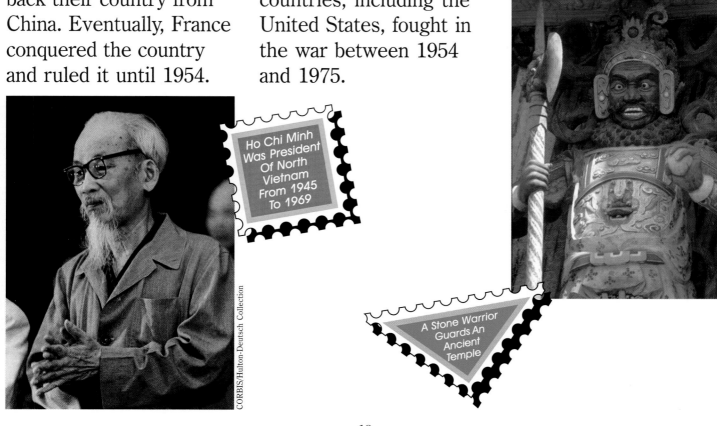

Ho Chi Minh Was President Of North Vietnam From 1945 To 1969

A Stone Warrior Guards An Ancient Temple

CORBIS/Hulton-Deutsch Collection

Vietnam Today

ADMIT ONE · ADMIT ONE

Small Businesses Line Tu Do Street In Ho Chi Minh City

CORBIS/Nik Wheeler

Because of the war, Vietnam has a lot of problems. Most of the country has not been rebuilt since the war. Many of the factories and businesses were destroyed. This means that there are not enough services, jobs, and food for Vietnam's huge population. Many Vietnamese people have left their country hoping to make a better life someplace else.

However, the Vietnamese are a proud people, and most have stayed in their homeland. In the small villages and farms, many people are poor and have trouble buying food and clothing.

Today, the government of Vietnam is **communist**. This means that, unlike in the United States of America, the government owns all the property and industry. In the past few years, the government has decided to let a few Vietnamese people own small farms and businesses. The government is trying to help it's people, and life is getting better for some Vietnamese.

A Floating Restaurant In Hoi An

CORBIS/Roman Soumar

Hoi An

Ho Chi Minh City

A Young
Boy Plows
A Field

More People
Have Bicycles
And Motorcycles
Than Cars In
Ho Chi Minh City

NORTH
VIETNAM

Ho Chi Minh City
Phung Hiep

CORBIS/Caroline Penn

The People

A Muong Girl Working The Fields In North Vietnam

Although Vietnam is one of the most populated countries in the world, nine out of ten people living there have the same **ethnic** background. That means that they come from the same culture.

Because people have been living in Vietnam for thousands of years, the Vietnamese have a strongly developed culture. In this culture, home and family are very important. Many relatives live in the same house, and they all look to the grandparents for rules and advice.

A Merchant Preparing Food In A Phung Hiep Floating Market

The population of Vietnam is getting bigger. This means that a lot of Vietnam's people are young. In fact, one out of every three people in Vietnam is a child.

ADMIT ONE

City Life
And
Country
Life

ADMIT ONE

A Traditional Muong House In The Hills At Hoa Binh

Life in the Vietnamese countryside has not changed for many generations. One of the special features about rural Vietnam is the village markets. In fact, in certain places in Vietnam, the markets float on the river. The "shops" are really boats that float along. People paddle smaller boats to the "shops" to buy their goods.

Vietnamese boats are called **sampans,** canoes, or "junks."

The markets are open only on certain days. In these markets, not only can you find food, clothes, and other supplies, but you can also see people in fancy clothes, dancing and singing beautiful songs.

A Boat On The Way To Phung Hiep Floating Market

18

Tony Roberts/Corbis

Hoa Binh

Ho Chi Minh City

Phung Hiep

Downtown
Ho Chi Minh
City At Dusk

☆ Ha Noi

• Ho Chi Minh City

A Young Girl
Studies At A
Desk Behind
Her Mother's
Bakery In
Ha Noi

Learning is very important to the Vietnamese. Students are expected to be very serious in school. Because of this, games are not often played in school, and each day begins with a test. Vietnamese schools do not have playground equipment, either. Another difference about school in Vietnam is that the students go to school even on Saturday.

When you go to a school in Vietnam, you will hear people speaking Vietnamese, the official language of the country. In the cities, you can hear people speaking Chinese, Russian, and English. If you go to the smaller villages, you can also hear people speaking ancient languages just as their relatives did hundreds of years ago.

CORBIS/Keren Su

Class Portrait Of Teenage Girls Wearing Ao Dais Dresses And Non La Hats

CORBIS/Owen Franken

A Business Language School In Ho Chi Minh City

Work

A Young Girl Carries Baskets Of Salt At A Salt Mine In Sa Huynh

CORBIS/Enzo & Paolo Ragazzini

In the country, most Vietnamese people are farmers. The most important crop in Vietnam is wet rice. To grow rice, the **paddy**, or field, must always be wet—or even completely under water! Growing rice is very hard because most of the work in the paddy is done by hand in the hot, wet weather. To protect themselves from the sun, the Vietnamese farmers wear a ***non la***, a large, cone-shaped straw hat.

Children Making Firecrackers In A Fireworks Factory In Da Nang

In the city, you can find people working in restaurants, shops, and factories. The people of Vietnam make everything from clothes and furniture to plastics and machines.

CORBIS/Michael Freeman

Halong
Bay

• Da Nang

Sa Huynh •

CORBIS/Catherine Karnow

A Young Girl
Sells Crabs
At A Floating
Fishing
Village In
Halong Bay

Merchants Sell Produce From Small Boats At A Floating Market At Can Tho

• Bac Ha

• Can Tho

Food

Vietnam is full of unusual and delicious foods. You can find meals made from cobra, bat, and eel, as well as more traditional meals of fish and vegetables. The main food of Vietnam, however, is rice. Most meals include rice.

A common Vietnamese food is *pho* (FO). This is a spicy noodle soup made with different types of meat. Vietnamese people also eat a great deal of vegetables and fruits. Some are common, like bananas and pineapples, while others have names like "star apples" and "green dragons."

CORBIS/Jeremy Horner

A Muong Girl Eating Pho Soup For Lunch In Bac Ha

To the Vietnamese, the most important drink is tea. They drink hot tea in the winter and cold tea in the summer. People of all ages drink tea at breakfast, lunch, and supper.

A Girl Cooking Stuffed Leaves Over A Trough Of Embers

CORBIS/Tim Page

Pastimes and Holidays

ADMIT ONE

ADMIT ONE

Many Vietnamese people play sports. You can find people playing volleyball or tennis, fishing, or simply swimming in the ocean water. The most popular sport in Vietnam is soccer. Most of the large cities have their own soccer team, and people can watch the matches for free.

Besides sports, Vietnamese people like to travel to the many interesting places in their country. In Vietnam, they can hike in the mountains, study 100 year-old buildings in the cities, or lie on the warm beaches of the coast.

One of the biggest holidays in Vietnam is the Vietnamese New Year. This holiday lasts for many days and has a lot of interesting traditions. During these days, people celebrate with food, parades, and fireworks. All over Vietnam, smaller holidays are also celebrated. During these days, people enjoy music, dancing, and games.

Whether you like games and parades or quiet nights and exciting days, Vietnam has something for everyone. From the beaches to the mountains, Vietnam will be a place you will never forget!

Boys Play Soccer On The Beach In Nha Trang

An Elephant Race In Buon Ma Thuot

CORBIS/Tim Page

CORBIS/Steve Raymer

A Religious Service Inside Cao Dai Cathedral In Tay Ninh

Area
About 128,000 square miles (332,000 square kilometers)—about the size of Iowa and Missouri combined.

Population
More than 79 million people.

Capitol City
Ha Noi.

Other Important Cities
Ho Chi Minh City, Da Nang, Da Lat, and Hue.

Money
The dong.

National Language
Vietnamese.

National Song
"Tien Quoc Ca," or "The Troops are Advancing."

National Holiday
National Day on September 2-3.

National Flag
A solid red square with a large gold star in the middle. The red color and the star stand for the communist revolution that led to Vietnam's type of government.

Heads of Government
The president and prime minister of Vietnam.